A CENTURY *of*
NORWICH

The famous figures of Samson and Hercules have stood guard either side of the doorway of this ancient merchant's house on Tombland for over 200 years. The building has a chequered past. It was built on the site of Sir John Fastolf's manor house by Christopher Jay to 'signalise his Mayoralty of Norwich' in 1657. The figures were placed outside the door in about 1789. The building was restored by its owner, noted antiquarian George Cubitt, at the end of the nineteenth century and later sold and became a YWCA in 1924. In 1934 Teddy Bush bought the building and developed it into a dance hall which could convert into a swimming pool, known simply as 'Samson & Hercules House'. For the last 50 years it has been solely used as a nightclub. During the war years the establishment was nicknamed 'The Muscle Men' after its doorway guardians. In 1993 the figures were removed for conservation owing to their great age and acts of vandalism inflicted on them. In April 1999 fibreglass replicas of the familiar guardsmen of Tombland were installed in place of the originals which are due to be put on display in the newly refurbished Castle Museum in 2001.

A CENTURY *of*
NORWICH

NEIL R. STOREY

SUTTON PUBLISHING

First published in the United Kingdom in 2000 by Sutton Publishing Limited

This new paperback edition first published in 2007 by
Sutton Publishing, an imprint of NPI Media Group
Cirencester Road · Chalford · Stroud · Gloucestershire · GL6 8PE

British Library Cataloguing in Publication Data
A catalogue record for this book is available from the British Library.

ISBN 978-0-7509-4897-5

Front endpaper: Norwich Castle and Cattle Market, *c.* 1906.
Back endpaper: Norwich City Hall and Market, 2000.
Half title page: Norwich Cathedral, *c.* 1910.
Title page: Richard Hearne, TV's 'Mr Pastry', visits the city where he was born, *c.* 1960.

This book is dedicated, with love, to my son Lawrence
'You don't always have to make changes to really
make a difference.'   (Old saying)

Typeset in Photina.
Typesetting and origination by
Sutton Publishing.
Printed and bound in England.

Contents

An intrigued crowd lines Prince of Wales Road to watch the grand entrance of Barnum & Bailey's Circus into Norwich, 29 July 1899.

Britain: A Century
of Change

Two women encumbered with gas masks go about their daily tasks during
the early days of the war. (*Hulton Getty Picture Collection*)

The sixty years ending in 1900 were a period of huge trans-
formation for Britain. Railway stations, post-and-telegraph offices,
police and fire stations, gasworks and gasometers, new livestock
markets and covered markets, schools, churches, football grounds,
hospitals and asylums, water pumping stations and sewerage plants
totally altered the urban scene, and the country's population tripled
with more than seven out of ten people being born in or moving to the
towns. The century that followed, leading up to the Millennium's end in
2000, was to be a period of even greater change.

When Queen Victoria died in 1901, she was measured for her
coffin by her grandson Kaiser Wilhelm, the London prostitutes put on
black mourning and the blinds came down in the villas and terraces
spreading out from the old town centres. These centres were reachable
by train and tram, by the new bicycles and still newer motor cars,
were connected by the new telephone, and lit by gas or even electricity.
The shops may have been full of British-made cotton and woollen
clothing but the grocers and butchers were selling cheap Danish
bacon, Argentinian beef, Australasian mutton and tinned or dried
fish and fruit from Canada, California and South Africa. Most of these
goods were carried in British-built-and-crewed ships burning Welsh
steam coal.

As the first decade moved on, the Open Spaces Act meant more
parks, bowling greens and cricket pitches. The First World War
transformed the place of women, as they took over many men's jobs.
Its other legacies were the war memorials which joined the statues of
Victorian worthies in main squares round the land. After 1918 death
duties and higher taxation bit hard, and a quarter of England changed
hands in the space of only a few years.

The multiple shop – the chain store – appeared in the high street:
Sainsburys, Maypole, Lipton's, Home & Colonial, the Fifty Shilling
Tailor, Burton, Boots, W.H. Smith. The shopper was spoilt for choice,
attracted by the brash fascias and advertising hoardings for national
brands like Bovril, Pears Soap, and Ovaltine. Many new buildings
began to be seen, such as garages, motor showrooms, picture palaces
(cinemas), 'palais de dance', and ribbons of 'semis' stretched along the
roads and new bypasses and onto the new estates nudging the green
belts.

During the 1920s cars became more reliable and sophisticated as well
as commonplace, with developments like the electric self-starter making
them easier for women to drive. Who wanted to turn a crank handle
in the new short skirt? This was, indeed, the electric age as much as
the motor era. Trolley buses, electric trams and trains extended mass
transport and electric light replaced gas in the street and the home,
which itself was groomed by the vacuum cleaner.

A major jolt to the march onward and upward was administered by the Great Depression of the early 1930s. The older British industries – textiles, shipbuilding, iron, steel, coal – were already under pressure from foreign competition when this worldwide slump arrived. Luckily there were new diversions to alleviate the misery. The 'talkies' arrived in the cinemas; more and more radios and gramophones were to be found in people's homes; there were new women's magazines, with fashion, cookery tips and problem pages; football pools; the flying feats of women pilots like Amy Johnson; the Loch Ness Monster; cheap chocolate and the drama of Edward VIII's abdication.

Things were looking up again by 1936 and new light industry was booming in the Home Counties as factories struggled to keep up with the demand for radios, radiograms, cars and electronic goods, including the first television sets. The threat from Hitler's Germany meant rearmament, particularly of the airforce, which stimulated aircraft and aero engine firms. If you were lucky and lived in the south, there was good money to be earned. A semi-detached house cost £450, a Morris Cowley £150. People may have smoked like chimneys but life expectancy, since 1918, was up by 15 years while the birth rate had almost halved.

A W.H. Smith shop front in Beaconsfield, 1922.

In some ways it is the little memories that seem to linger longest from the second World War: the kerbs painted white to show up in the blackout, the rattle of ack-ack shrapnel on roof tiles, sparrows killed by bomb blast. The biggest damage, apart from London, was in the south-west (Plymouth, Bristol) and the Midlands (Coventry, Birmingham). Postwar reconstruction was rooted in the Beveridge Report which set out the expectations for the Welfare State. This, together with the nationalisation of the Bank of England, coal, gas, electricity and the railways, formed the programme of the Labour government in 1945.

Children collecting aluminium to help the war effort, London, 1940s. (*IWM*)

Times were hard in the late 1940s, with rationing even more stringent than during the war. Yet this was, as has been said, 'an innocent and well-behaved era'. The first let-up came in 1951 with the Festival of Britain and there was another fillip in 1953 from the Coronation, which incidentally gave a huge boost to the spread of TV. By 1954 leisure motoring had been resumed but the Comet – Britain's best hope for taking on the American aviation industry – suffered a series of mysterious crashes. The Suez debacle of 1956 was followed by an acceleration in the withdrawal from Empire, which had begun in 1947 with the Independence of India. Consumerism was truly born with the advent of commercial TV and most homes soon boasted washing machines, fridges, electric irons and fires.

A street party to celebrate the Queen's Coronation, June 1953. (*Hulton Getty Picture Collection*)

The *Lady Chatterley* obscenity trial in 1960 was something of a straw in the wind for what was to follow in that decade. A collective loss of inhibition seemed to sweep the land, as the Beatles and the Rolling Stones transformed popular music, and retailing, cinema and the theatre were revolutionised. Designers, hairdressers, photographers and models moved into places vacated by an Establishment put to flight by the new breed of satirists spawned by *Beyond the Fringe* and *Private Eye*.

In the 1970s Britain seems to have suffered a prolonged hangover after the excesses of the previous decade. Ulster,

inflation and union troubles were not made up
for by entry into the EEC, North Sea Oil, Women's
Lib or, indeed, Punk Rock. Mrs Thatcher applied
the corrective in the 1980s, as the country moved
more and more from its old manufacturing base
over to providing services, consulting, advertising, and expertise in the 'invisible' market of high
finance or in IT.

The post-1945 townscape has seen changes
to match those in the worlds of work, entertainment and politics. In 1952 the Clean Air Act
served notice on smogs and pea-souper fogs, smuts
and blackened buildings, forcing people to stop
burning coal and go over to smokeless sources of
heat and energy. In the same decade some of the
best urban building took place in the 'new towns'
like Basildon, Crawley, Stevenage and Harlow.
Elsewhere open warfare was declared on slums
and what was labelled inadequate, cramped, back-
to-back, two-up, two-down, housing. The new
'machine for living in' was a flat in a high-rise
block. The architects and planners who promoted
these were in league with the traffic engineers,
determined to keep the motor car moving
whatever the price in multi-storey car parks,
meters, traffic wardens and ring roads. The old
pollutant, coal smoke, was replaced by petrol and
diesel exhaust, and traffic noise.

Punk rockers demonstrate their anarchic style during
the 1970s. (*Barnaby's Picture Library*)

Fast food was no longer only a pork pie in a pub or fish-and-chips.
There were Indian curry houses, Chinese take-aways and American-
style hamburgers, while the drinker could get away from beer in a
wine bar. Under the impact of television the big Gaumonts and Odeons
closed or were rebuilt as multi-screen cinemas, while the palais de
dance gave way to discos and clubs.

From the late 1960s the introduction of listed buildings and conservation areas, together with the growth of preservation societies, put a
brake on 'comprehensive redevelopment'. The end of the century and
the start of the Third Millennium see new challenges to the health
of towns and the wellbeing of the nine out of ten people who now
live urban lives. The fight is on to prevent town centres from dying,
as patterns of housing and shopping change, and edge-of-town super-
markets exercise the attractions of one-stop shopping. But as banks
and department stores close, following the haberdashers, greengrocers,
butchers and ironmongers, there are signs of new growth such as

Millennium celebrations over the Thames
at Westminster, New Year's Eve, 1999.
(*Barnaby's Picture Library*)

farmers' markets, and corner stores acting as pick-up points where
customers collect shopping ordered on-line from web sites.

Futurologists tell us that we are in stage two of the consumer revolu-
tion: a shift from mass consumption to mass customisation driven by
a desire to have things that fit us and our particular lifestyle exactly,
and for better service. This must offer hope for small city-centre shop
premises, as must the continued attraction of physical shopping,
browsing and being part of a crowd: in a word, 'shoppertainment'.
Another hopeful trend for towns is the growth in the number of young
people postponing marriage and looking to live independently, alone,
where there is a buzz, in 'swinging single cities'. Theirs is a 'flats-and-
cafés' lifestyle, in contrast to the 'family suburbs', and certainly fits in
with government's aim of building 60 per cent of the huge amount of
new housing needed on 'brown' sites, recycled urban land. There looks
to be plenty of life in the British town yet.

Norwich: An Introduction

With the coming of a new century imaginations are fired to create new ideas covering all aspects of the practical, moral and emancipated structure of our life and surroundings for the perceived good of the future. Norwich was to see some of the greatest changes, destruction, improvement, innovation and upheavals in its entire history enacted during the twentieth century.

In 1900 Norwich, with its population of 111,733 souls, was still more or less contained within its medieval walls which had been built to contain a city of about 5,000 citizens. Its roads were narrow and twisty, many of them unmade or in a poor state of repair. Large areas of the city were described as '. . . some of the most disgraceful slums in England' where families crammed themselves into cramped and poorly maintained housing based around the 749 courts and yards in the city. Many of them had no sanitation with heaps of human dung, up to 9 feet across, recorded in the yards where disease was as rife as the misery therein.

The only road of 'modern' construction which affected the medieval pattern was Prince of Wales Road. Opened in November 1862, it was built on the back gardens of once fashionable houses as a commercial speculation to link Thorpe station by means of a grand boulevard to the city centre. Sadly the project ran out of money but Alexandra Mansions (1865) and the summit area around Agricultural Hall Plain – including Hardwick House (1866), Agricultural Hall (1882) and the Royal Hotel (1897) – demonstrate some of the planned grand architecture proposed for the scheme.

The Norwich Electric Tramways Act came into force in July 1897. The company, which had a total capital of £240,000 paid up in £10 shares, began purchasing property in the city according to the powers granted by the Act. Another Act (1898) for the improvement of the city streets meant a number of slums were removed and roads were widened and made up with pathways. Together they enabled an efficient and effective tram system to begin operations in 1900. The overcrowding of the city began to be eased with this practical and cost-effective link between the growing 'New City' and the artisan suburbs of streets of terraced houses, corner shops and pubs outside the old walls, while the inner city retained its factories, larger shops and workforce!

Many products and businesses which were household names originated from Norwich: J & J Colman Ltd's Mustard and Starch, Wincarnis Tonic, Steward and Patteson, Morgans and Youngs, Crawshay & Youngs breweries, Barnard, Bishop & Barnard and Boulton & Paul engineers along with Caley's Mineral Water, Chocolates and Crackers were familiar businesses based in the city. The largest employers in the city were however the huge boot and shoe factories of companies like Howlett & White and Southall's (later known by the name of their most famous shoe 'Start-Rite'). By 1931, 10,800 Norwich people were employed in boot and shoe manufacture with twenty-six firms producing 6,000,000 pairs of shoes – 16 per cent of the total British output in 1935.

The factories not only provided employment but often included pastoral care and benefits such as sponsored housing, medical care schemes and schools for their employees. Each of these great businesses had their own unique sounds and smells and became so much part of the fabric of the city that it was thought they would last forever. Today Norwich's largest employers are found in the insurance industry; all of the others either no longer exist or have changed beyond recognition.

The peaceful status quo of the improving city was lost in 1914 when the country was plunged into war. Norwich answered the call of the war effort by sending thousands of men and women to serve king and country in all theatres of the war. Many businesses changed what they were doing or developed new products. Examples include Boulton & Paul who began military aircraft manufacture and Barnards who made self assembly buildings and barbed wire under contract to the War Office. Harmer's made uniforms, and the boot factories made footwear

Panoramic view of the city. *c.* 1925.

for our fighting forces. Even Caley's, with their experience of gunpowder for crackers, produced munitions.

Over 3,500 Norwich men and women were killed in the First World War. Of those who returned many were crippled in mind and body and disillusioned with the lack of a 'Land Fit for Heroes' promised for their return. Many were reduced to selling rags and matches on the Market. Things were never quite the same again.

Norwich City Council did want to make things better for those who had returned from war. A concerted effort was made to give employment to city men by starting a major building programme in 1918 when construction began on the Mile Cross Housing Estate, the first council housing estate in the country.

The yard of the Bess of Bedlam public house, 80 Oak Street, *c.* 1903. The landlord at the time was Robert John Arturton who was also a successful general carter and contractor.

All of the thirty public parks, gardens and recreation grounds which surround the city – a total of more than 738 acres – were created or improved during the 1920s and '30s. It is not surprising that, by the late 1920s, the Labour Party became the largest group on the city council and gained complete control in 1933.

From this time on the most significant of all the development projects were undertaken. In 1928 the council began purchasing houses all around the municipal buildings and St Peter's Road area. Following a number of reports and a competition to select a designer and architects, work began on the construction of the new city hall in 1936.

In a project which cost over £200,000 the old city Market Place was completely redesigned and crowned with new civic buildings, which have been described as 'the best example of inter-war years municipal architecture in the country'.

During the Second World War the city and its people answered the call again but this time the war came to the city. Norwich residents had experienced bombing raids since 1940 but nothing prepared them for the blitz of April 1942, known as the 'Baedeker Blitz'. The Luftwaffe were given orders to bomb targets of historical significance in an attempt to break British morale. Norwich citizens were killed as a result of the bombing raids, and large areas of the city were reduced to burnt out shells or piles of wood and rubble.

Out of the ashes of the blitz rose a plan which threatened to put paid to most of what was left of the historical city of Norwich. The Norwich City Plan of 1946 included inner and outer ring roads, new housing developments and a grand plan for a large 'open plaza'-style civic centre.

Luckily the City Plan was considered over a 25-year period and the sweeping changes to the city centre were not carried out entirely. In the 1960s, however, the construction of the inner ring road saw whole areas of the city which had survived the blitz put asunder by the demolition gangs. Historic areas like Grapes Hill, Chapel Field, Magdalen Street and St Stephens were knocked about or given 'features' which have irreparably damaged or destroyed the area as we knew it. It was also during this time that some hideous office blocks which still aggrieve our skyline were erected.

Children crowd on to Orford Hill to watch a Saturday afternoon Punch & Judy show. *c.* 1906.

Time has marched on and Norwich people are now given a greater voice in deciding the shape and future of major developments in the city. The old cattle market area was redeveloped to become the Castle Mall Shopping Centre, which opened in 1993. From the mid-1990s the city's riverside has been developed from old engineering works, factories and wharves into a trendy area for arts and entertainment with additional parking. A number of the grand Victorian breweries, along with the old boot and shoe factories, have not been demolished but have been converted to offices or smart residential accommodation.

Following the terrible fire at the library and the sell-off of the Nestlé site, redevelopment of the Chapel Field and Bethel Street areas has involved a number of public presentations and a great deal of serious consultation with the people of Norwich. As we advance into the twenty-first century I look forward to seeing the new library and Chapelfield area develop. I simply hope the sites will be as sympathetic and beneficial to the city as they are promised to be.

Finally, I raise a glass to the fine old City of Norwich, the city which could once truthfully claim 'a pub for every day and a church for every weekend' – we're not too far out even today. We have a lot to be proud of but also need to remember what we've lost; we must not forget or become complacent about the historical buildings we are blessed with and could take for granted as part of our city. It is up to us to be responsible for what is left of Norwich's past for its future. As the Norfolk saying goes when you are entrusted with a treasured heirloom: 'Now, dew yew maik sure an' tek care of ut!'

Neil R. Storey
Norwich, 2000

The Start of the Century

A dancing bear and his keeper on Earlham Road, 1900.

At the turn of the twentieth century Norwich was a city seeing unprecedented change; a tram system was being installed across the city. Here one of the labourers with his 'barra' carts some of the rubble from St Andrews Street, *c.* 1898. An old inn known as The City Arms was demolished in order to make a new road for the trams from Redwell Street into St Andrew's Broad Street and so on to Charing Cross, St Benedicts and Dereham Road.

Once the roadways were knocked through, the tram tracks were laid. Here on St Stephen's Street we see the double tram tracks being laid in 1899. The tram system comprised a total of 19 miles, 2 furlongs and 100 yards of rails.

The tram terminus at Orford Place shortly after its official opening on 30 July 1900. As the overcrowded Victorian city spread further beyond its ancient walls and boundaries, trams were seen as an efficient and cost-effective means of transport. Accordingly tram routes were rapidly extended to the growing suburbs on Unthank Road, City Road, Aylsham Road and to Trowse station.

Tram no. 30's driver and conductor pause for the photographer while on their route between Thorpe Road, Christchurch Road and Newmarket Road on the Norwich Tramway, *c.* 1901.

Norwich Market Place, *c.* 1899. Taken shortly before the tram lines were laid this image shows the uneven lines of market stalls which were set up and taken down every day, leaving the Market Place a clean and open vista for civic occasions. To the left is the statue of the Duke of Wellington erected in 1854. In the foreground are the carriers, carts and waggons which took people and goods from the outlying villages to and from the market.

Viewing Prince of Wales Road from Agricultural Hall Plain in about 1903 we can get an idea of what the planned 'Grand Boulevard' to impress rail travellers arriving at Thorpe station and visiting the city would have looked like. Its construction began in the 1860s when Prince of Wales Road was cut through the gardens of houses backing on to the proposed route. The great buildings included Alexandra Mansions (the city's first flats, 1865), the Agricultural Hall (1882), the Crown Bank (now Anglia TV) and the Royal Hotel opened in 1897. Like many good schemes this one ran out of money after about a quarter of the plan was carried out; the rest was never completed.

This crowded Norwich street scene shows one of the once familiar sights of the summer months as children set out on their Sunday School Treat from Mousehold Street. *c.* 1904. With a church for every week of the year and a host of non-conformist chapels across the city, many children joined more than one Sunday School so they got to go on more than one annual treat.

R. Mann's hot potato and pie cart, just one of the many carts which plied their wares along the streets of Norwich at the turn of the century. This particular cart was no doubt unique as it was built to look like a railway engine. Constructed by the notable city manufacturing ironmongers Johnson, Burton & Theobald of West Pottergate, the main body of the 'engine' was a large oven where the pies were kept hot while the potatoes were roasted in the firebox and then transferred to the oven.

21

Lord Avebury gives the address after he unveiled the statue of the great scholar Sir Thomas Browne, author of *Religio Medici*, 19 October 1905. This fine statue, by Henry Pegram, would have faced Sir Thomas's old house but it was sadly demolished in the road widening scheme for trams in 1900. The statue still stands today although the fine little park which surrounded it on Hay Hill has now been paved over.

Plucking swans at the Great Hospital, *c.* 1905. In the past the flesh of the cygnet was greatly esteemed as a delicacy of the gentry's table. In Norfolk many of the old-established families were allowed to claim their swans by nicking a mark in the birds' beak during the upping season. The Great Hospital was also permitted to keep swans and had a swan pit to fatten the birds from medieval times. This practice was continued until the Second World War when it ceased because grain could no longer be spared for the purpose.

Evening News paperboys on their free trip to the Hippodrome, 1905. When this photo was taken few of these boys would have delivered papers to your door; they would have stood on street corners across the city with a large bag of papers strung around their neck. The banner headlines would have been printed on a large sheet hung off the bag, and the boys would have called out the headlines and which edition of the paper they were selling.

Parents who wished their daughters to obtain positions in the 'better' households could, after their little girl attained the age of 14, seek a reference from their local Rector to send her to the Norwich School of Cookery and Domestic Science. This was situated in Colegate and was run by Headmistress Lucy Parnell. If the girl passed her entrance tests she would be admitted and given three months' training in the art of the domestic servant including machine sewing, bodice making, cooking, polishing and hygiene. Pictured here are some of the girls at a cake-making class, *c.* 1905.

Children crowd together for the photographer at the Tombland Fair, *c.* 1905. Recorded as early as the twelfth century, the name of the fair has become something of a misnomer as it has not actually been held on Tombland since 1818 when it was moved by local bylaw following complaints from residents about the prolonged noise and disruption. For many years thereafter it was held on the site of the Cattle Market near the castle. Since this area was developed for the Castle Mall the fair has suffered an itinerant existence between Castle Meadow and Chapel Field Gardens.

William Childerhouse, Norwich City Bellman or Town Crier from 1877 until his death in 1905, meets a travelling giant, *c.* 1905. Childerhouse began his working life as a hawker of mussels and watercress. His fine voice was noticed by the then editor of the fledgling *Eastern Daily Press* who employed him to sell the paper on a salary of 13s 4d per annum and also undertook ad hoc advertisement or electioneering calls set at 40 calls for half a crown and civic toastmastering for £5 per annum. It has been estimated that during his career as Bellman he cried 600,000 announcements and walked 70,000 miles.

Harry Moulton, the last Norwich City Corporation Bellman, photographed in front of the Dolphin Inn on Heigham Street with his dog Prince, *c.* 1906. He obtained the position after the death of William Childerhouse and held it until his office was abolished during the First World War when ringing bells warned of either invasion or air raids. This traditional post was resumed in 1986 when the great local character David Bullock was officially appointed Bellman or Town Crier to the city.

Large sections of City Wall, which were built on to by domestic housing, are revealed as Coburg Street was demolished to make way for the expanding Caley Factory, *c.* 1906. Coburg Street ran from St Stephen's to Chapel Field East. The houses on the other side of the wall were badly damaged in the air raids of 1942. Eventually they were demolished and cleared to make way for the inner link road dual carriageway in the 1960s.

Building a fine home for 'The Canaries': we see 'The Nest' under construction in April 1908. Norwich City Football Club was formed in 1902; their original playing ground was on Newmarket Road. In 1908 they moved to their first purpose-built ground here in the old chalk pit on Rosary Road. The first match at the ground resulted in a 2–1 win for City against Fulham in a friendly match on 1 September 1908.

The burnt-out shell of the Cock Inn at Old Lakenham, 31 March 1908. The fire was caused by sparks being carried on the high winds from the raging blaze at Lakenham Mill catching on the thatched roof. The old pub was soon well ablaze and the fire eventually not only gutted the inn but also the adjacent house. It was rebuilt in its traditional style and is still serving today.

The tower of the Roman Catholic church nears completion, 1909. Built between 1884 and 1910 it was financed by the 15th Duke of Norfolk. It stands on the site of the old City of Norwich Gaol and is 81 feet high inside the chancel. The church was given cathedral status by the Vatican on 13 March 1976; its bishop was enthroned on 2 June the same year.

Billy Bluelight, probably the most famous of all Norwich characters, was born William
Cullum in 1859. In the winter months he would travel door to door or stand by
the Royal Arcade, in his 'uniform' of shiny peaked cap and military-style frock coat
festooned with medallions and badges, selling cough sweets. He will, however, be best
remembered for his antics in the summer months. When rigged out as we see him here
he would race the SS *Jenny Lind* from Foundry Bridge to Thorpe Reach and even Great
Yarmouth. As he ran he called out 'My name is Billy Bluelight, my age is forty-five,
I hope to get to Carrow Bridge before the boat arrive.' The river boat was always full of
fascinated travellers who would tip Billy by putting money into his doffed, outheld cap
as he waited at the end of the gangplank. Billy Bluelight died on 10 July 1949, aged
ninety. A bench was erected by public subscription in his memory and even a pub on
Hall Road was re-christened the Billy Bluelight in his honour in the 1990s.

On parade, marching past the Royal Hotel are members of the Norwich City Salvation Army, the Boys' Brigade and the Friends First Day Schools, *c.* 1910. Before the days of radios and television in every house parades and street processions were common features of Norwich life. In those days most groups had their own band or corps of drums. Many such groups were based around a religious or charitable organisation often meeting at the 'tin tabernacle' or wooden chapel at the bottom of the street.

The future Sir Henry Jerningham (Lord Stafford) in his black frock coat and top hat pauses for the camera along with his wife who is holding her parasol. Their entourage of cars, in front of the now demolished Costessey Hall, makes ready to take two African dignitaries (seated in the rear of the front car) on a tour around Norfolk. In 1910 cars were a rare enough sight on the road but three in procession, one containing African visitors in full ethnic regalia, was unheard of. Their progress around the county was captured by many local photographers and was sold in the form of souvenir postcards.

Edward VII in his carriage with escort of outriders from the King's Own Royal Regiment Norfolk Yeomanry during his visit to Norwich on 25 October 1909. Having presented colours and inspected local territorial battalions and members of the Royal Norfolk Veterans Association, he is seen leaving Mousehold Heath, sung on his way by the voices of 11,000 schoolchildren who cover the hillside.

Walter Rye, Norfolk antiquarian, 1834–1929. Although his interests extended across the county I can think of nobody of his time who did more by their single efforts to preserve, research and record the intrinsic character and ancient buildings of the City of Norwich. He was the last Mayor of Norwich; he always claimed 'the old plain Mayoralty of Norwich was more honourable than a later-given Lord Mayorship'. It fell during his mayoralty that Edward VII, a stickler for etiquette at public occasions, visited the city. To the dismay of the town clerk and other local dignitaries Walter Rye insisted on receiving the King in his customary tweeds!

Dr Bertram Pollock, Bishop of Norwich from 1910 to 1942. Born at Wimbledon in 1863 to a family famous in the law he was assistant master at Marlborough College before he was ordained in 1891. Appointed to the Norwich Bishopric in 1910 he was always a well-respected and prominent Bishop closely involved with all strata of Norfolk society, particularly those involved in agriculture. Among his many works he was conspicuous in the attempts to secure settlement of the Norfolk Farm Labourers' strike in 1923. In the 1930s he held services at holiday camps and once had a congregation of 4,000 at a service in a circus where the ringmaster read the lesson. He died peacefully at his home at Gissing in 1943, just a year after his retirement as Bishop of Norwich.

A huge crowd packs the market square in front of the old municipal buildings to hear the Lord Mayor of Norwich, Dr Ernest Edward Blyth, deliver the Proclamation of HM King George V's accession to the throne on 9 May 1910. Dr Blyth was the city's first Lord Mayor after the 'Civic Knighthood' was conferred by Edward VII on 24 February 1910.

On Coronation Day, 22 June 1911, Norwich celebrated in style. After church services and a grand procession at the cathedral, street parties were held across the city. The culmination of events was a grand fireworks display crowned by the ignition of a 30 foot bonfire, on Mousehold Heath, a gift of the Lord Mayor.

A few days after his coronation King George V made his first official visit to Norwich on 28 June 1911. The streets were decked with bunting and these distinctive Arches of Triumph were erected along London Street. Many of the shops were decked with flags and thousands lined the route as the king was driven through the city in his carriage. After a reception in St Andrew's Hall and a civic welcome in the Market Place His Majesty finished his day with a visit to the Royal Norfolk Show, held that year at Crown Point, Trowse.

lying over the heads of the expectant crowd on 10 August 1912 is pioneering and daredevil aviator Bentfield C. Hucks in
is *Daily Mail*-sponsored Blériot monoplane 'Firefly'. He is seen completing the last leg of his momentous journey from Crow
all Farm, Gorleston, to Church Lane, Eaton; his achievement being that on this flight he was the first man to fly over the
ity of Norwich.

Typifying the way Norwich people react to adversity with good old Norfolk humour lads congregate to look at the rare sight of the city streets under flood. The photo was taken on Barn Road shortly after Monday 26 August 1912, the day of the 'tidal wave' which swept through the city when the Wensum burst its banks. Over 7.5 inches of rain and unusually high tides combined to create the disaster which caused over £100,000 of damage and 15,000 lost homes or property across the county.

Herbert Batson on the no. 11 Norwich Corporation water cart near St Olave's Road, *c.* 1912. Even when the rows of new terraced houses were being built at the turn of the century it did not guarantee the houses would be equipped with indoor flush toilets or piped water. In some areas the water quality from the yard pumps was judged so bad that the corporation took around carts of drinking water which could be purchased at a ha'penny a bucket.

The Norwich Electric Theatre, 102–104 Prince of Wales Road shortly after its opening on 26 December 1912. This beautiful building was designed by Francis Burdett Ward and was the forerunner of many cinema designs. When 'talkies' came to this cinema in April 1929, 89,000 people came to see *Sunny Side Up* during its five week run. Re-christened the Norvic in 1949, it lasted twelve more years until it was demolished in 1961.

George Chamberlin, Chairman of Norwich City Chamber of Trade, is seen facing us in the rear seat of the carriage as he and the visiting delegates leave Norwich Cathedral for the Castle on 22 June 1914. The delegates were part of a large party of French and Belgian editors and litterateurs on a tour of British holiday resorts as the guests of the Federation of British Health and Holiday Resorts to promote the attractions of our country to holidaymakers in Europe. It is rather ironic that over the next few years many British service personnel saw tours of France and Belgium they would never want to repeat.

A group of 'Borrovians' gather for the camera at the opening of the Borrow House Museum on 5 July 1913. This little house on Willow Lane was home, from 1816 to 1824, to the great Norfolk author George Borrow (1803–81). Borrow wrote *The Bible in Spain*, *Romany Rye* and his classic *Lavengro*. The museum was presented to the Corporation of the City of Norwich by Arthur Michael Samuel MP (later Lord Mancroft) during his Lord Mayoralty in 1913. By the generosity of Mr William Thomas Fisher Jarrold, and with donations from other Borrovians, the house was furnished in the style of the period. The little museum was enjoyed by many at 6*d* a visit but sadly as time went on it became forgotten. It is now a council house marked with a plaque and those in authority are 'not quite sure' where all its contents are today.

General Sir Robert Baden Powell leads the cheers at the end of his much-heralded visit to review over 2,000 local scouts at Crown Point, Trowse on Saturday 20 June 1914. On a day which enjoyed the best of summer weather, the occasion featured a field of activities and displays inspected by Sir Robert as well as special presentations of Scout badges and awards, capped off with the presentation of a pennant to the Wroxham troop.

The
First World War

On the eve of war the boys from 'Carrow Artillery', part of the 1st
East Anglian Brigade Royal Field Artillery, gather for a last drink with
workmates at Colman's Carrow Works Club House before going to their
war stations, August 1914.

Reserve soldiers of the Norfolk Regiment make ready to leave for war from Thorpe station, August 1914. The 1st Battalion was the only Regular Army Battalion of our county regiment to fight in France and Flanders. They were well reinforced by local volunteers throughout the war and were joined on the Western Front in 1915 by the 7th, 8th and 9th (Service) Battalions. Between them they were to be present at most of the significant actions through the campaign.

The Chapel Field Drill Hall, *c.* 1914. This grand old building was opened in October 1866 by HRH the Prince of Wales as a headquarters for the various Norwich volunteer units. From 1908 it was the headquarters of the 4th Battalion, the Norfolk Regiment. From here the battalion which comprised companies from Norwich, Diss, Attleborough and District, Wymondham, Thetford and Thorpe mobilised for war in August 1914. Throughout the war hundreds of local lads walked through the doors of this building which was festooned with flags and eye-catching, colourful recruiting posters of the day, to join the colours and take their attestation here. The Drill Hall, with all its history, was demolished to make way for the inner link road in 1963.

After war was declared at 11 p.m. on 4 August 1914 the men of the 4th Battalion the Norfolk Regiment reported the following morning to the Drill Hall on Chapel Field. Because the battalion numbered about 1,000 men who came from the various companies in and around Norwich they needed somewhere to stay so the City of Norwich Schools on Newmarket Road were commandeered as billets. These are some of the men in front of the school as the sergeants check their company muster rolls.

Men of the XII (Prince of Wales's Royal) Lancers trot up the siding at Thorpe station ready to embark on their train which would transport both the men and the horses to France on 16 August 1914. The XII Lancers had been stationed at The Cavalry Barracks since 1912 and, by the time they mobilised for war in 1914, many Norwich men had joined their ranks. After a distinguished service throughout the war the Lancers earned battle honours for such engagements at Mons, Marne, Ypres, Arras, Cambrai, Somme and Sambre. Many men of the XIIth Lancers returned to their beloved Norwich where they had an active Old Comrades Association for many years.

New recruits for the 4th Battalion, the Norfolk Regiment, some of them risking a smile and a look for the camera, are put through their paces on a march down Earlham Road, 1914. About 1,400 men from Norwich and across the south and east of the country were raised for the battalion in the first four weeks of the war. The opening campaign in Gallipoli was to be the fate of the 4th and 5th Territorial Battalions of the Norfolk Regiment followed by campaigns in Egypt and Mesopotamia. It is quite possible that not one man in this photograph reached the end of the war without illness or injury; many of them never came home again.

Volunteers for Kitchener's Army 'enjoying' a physical training session on Chapel Field Gardens, 1914. These were men who had answered the call of the famous poster 'Your King and Country Need You' with Lord Kitchener's imposing finger and piercing eyes which called for 'K1', his first 100,000 men to enlist. There were not enough uniforms or fatigues to go round so they did their basic training in their 'civvy' clothes. The other problem was accommodation for all these new recruits. All the local barracks were full so many ended up sleeping under just a blanket in front of Britannia Barracks on Mousehold Heath.

Officers and men of the 2nd Battalion the Essex Regiment in Thorpe station yard, 10 August 1914. From August 1914 the recruits of the British Isles were pushed around the country like a great Chinese puzzle. As soon as a battalion of any county regiment had been raised for active service the War Office wanted them moved out of their home county to avoid soldiers sloping off to see friends and family after a day's training or at weekends. They wanted the men to work together as an army unit, building up solidarity by training and suffering with each other. As a result most of the Norfolk service battalions ended up at Shorncliffe and soldiers of the Essex Regiment (not to mention a diverse selection of battalions from as far apart as Scotland, Yorkshire and Wales) came to Norfolk.

'Wait here while we find you somewhere to stay' is not something you normally say to a battalion of soldiers. However, with the city bursting with new recruits and every barracks full, the men of the 2nd Battalion the Essex Regiment waited patiently in Norwich Market Place for a suitable area of ground to be made available in August 1914. It was certainly a fine spectacle for the people of Norwich who ring the site chatting to the soldiers. The ice cream vendors did very well that day as did the Norwich barbers who brought their chairs out to give the soldiers shaves and military haircuts.

Members of Norfolk Voluntary Aid Detachment no. 15 on City station, *c.* 1917. These were the men of the Norwich Transport Company (British Red Cross Society) who handled the returned wounded and sick servicemen from the Norwich stations to the hospitals in the city. The Norfolk & Norwich Hospital along with the war hospitals at Lakenham and Thorpe were delivered 40,498 patients in 317 convoys throughout the war, all of which were managed by the volunteers of the Norwich Transport Company.

Removing stretcher cases to ambulances from the first hospital train to arrive in Norwich on 17 October 1914. Following the opening battles of the First World War at Mons, Marne and Ypres the British Expeditionary Force of August 1914 had been decimated. Thousands were killed and thousands more wounded; those who could be moved were sent 'back to Blighty'. Hospitals across England were rapidly crammed with wounded servicemen and the scheme proposed by the Joint War Committee of the British Red Cross Society and Order of St John of Jerusalem was enacted as manors, town and village halls became auxiliary war hospitals. The casualties seen here from the first of many such trains were sent to both the Norfolk & Norwich Hospital and Woodbastwick Auxiliary War Hospital.

The Eastern Daily Press Ward shortly after its opening on 11 February 1915. As yet more offensives were tackled the casualties grew at a horrifying rate. The demands on provincial hospitals exceeded their facilities so drastic measures and careful innovation were employed to meet needs. In Norwich we were lucky to have a number of engineering firms that manufactured wooden assembly buildings. They easily fabricated a building attached to the Norfolk & Norwich Hospital as a ward. The money for this project, £2,418 9s 4d was raised in four days in December 1914.

'Straighten those backs!' Sergeant Instructor Bokenham of The Norfolk Regiment gives the members of the City of Norwich Volunteer Training Corps (the First World War equivalent of the Local Defence Volunteers) their basic training in foot drill on their first parade in the Market Place on 15 December 1914.

Norfolk War Hospital, with some of its nurses and wounded troops, *c.* 1915. Ever greater demands were placed on the hospitals as the trenches merged into a stalemate of slaughter. Further emergency wards were erected in huts and tents at The Norfolk & Norwich Hospital. When this was still not enough, the Asylum at Thorpe had its patients transferred and formally opened as the Norfolk War Hospital in 1915. Even this hospital had to have tent wards, but the quality of care was not compromised. Recuperation rates were excellent for the 30,000 troops who passed through its 2,450 beds during the war.

Mobile section of the City of Norwich Volunteers at their Headquarters on King Street in 1915. The Volunteer Training Corps system was started and run on a totally ad hoc basis in each county in 1914. The War Office recognised the value of a home-based volunteer force to back up home fighting forces and adopted the volunteers in a more formal way in January 1915. From this time on they were provided with army fatigues as uniforms, War Office directives and regulations to abide by and weaponry was issued (albeit, very piecemeal at first). They were also given a new title and granted a formal cap badge – the City of Norwich Volunteers.

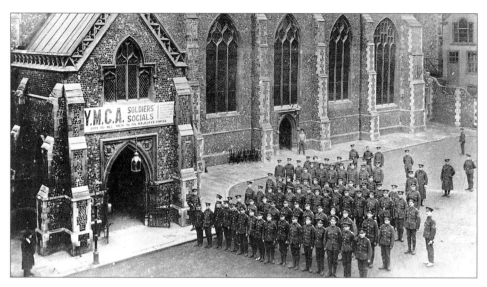

Members of the 2nd East Anglian Field Ambulance are seen on parade in front of St Andrew's Hall, *c.* 1916. Although an active service unit, there were always new recruits coming in through their headquarters on Bethel Street. Apart from the usual basic training in soldierly and medical skills they also helped run the funds for the YMCA, comforts funds and war hospitals. Such events would be attended by local people and a smattering of service personnel on leave, but often predominantly by the convalescent soldiers in their 'hospital blue' uniform.

Pipes and Drums of the 2/7th (Territorial) Battalion, Argyll & Sutherland Highlanders proudly march down Earlham Road as the Pipe Major, with his distinctive badger sporran, swings his mace, April 1917. Based at Taverham it was not long before the unusual sight of Scottish troops was seen in the city. The Scottish soldiers were sternly warned about the '. . . bold and dangerous mustard and vinegar factory girls who roamed the darkened streets in twos and threes looking in particular for a "kilty"'.

45

Munitions girls dressed in their 'National Shell' overalls, from Caley's St James's Works, *c*. 1916. Having handled gunpowder for the manufacture of Christmas crackers, the factory patriotically turned itself over to producing munitions. Girls had to take care because over exposure to cordite fumes tinged their hair ginger and their skin yellow, earning them the nickname of 'Norwich Canaries'. To recover their natural colour the girls would be sent by train to the coast to 'take the air'.

Boulton & Paul Ltd's Hangar and aircraft assembling plant on Mousehold, *c*. 1917. During the war Boulton & Paul was swamped with orders for all manner of military hardware such as huts, desert roadways, camouflage trellis and a total of 5,372 miles of wire netting for trench revetments. Their name, however, was to be made in aircraft. In October 1915 their first aircraft, an F.E.2b, flew from the newly laid out Mousehold airfield. Five hundred and fifty of these aircraft were turned out by Boulton & Paul and a total of 2,530 military airplanes including Sopwith Camels and Snipes were made by the company during the war. They also produced 7,835 propellers.

CSM Harry Daniels VC, 2nd Battalion the Rifle Brigade. He was Norfolk's first recipient of the Victoria Cross during the First World War. Born the thirteenth child of a trading couple on Market Street, Wymondham, in 1884 both his parents died when he was still a young lad. Put in the Boys' Home on St Faith's Lane, after a number of adventures he ran away to join the Rifle Brigade as a boy soldier. By 12 March 1915 he was a Company Sergeant Major. During the battle of Neuve Chapelle, he could see his battalion's advance would be hampered by the barbed wire entanglements in front of his trench. He cried 'Nobby get yer nippers' and he with Cpl 'Tom' Noble went over the top under severe machine gun fire to cut the wire. They were both wounded almost immediately but they carried on cutting. Poor Tom caught a shot to the chest but Harry managed to crawl back when the job was done. For their gallant actions they were both awarded our nation's highest award, the Victoria Cross. A few months later Harry Daniels returned to his beloved home county where he was given a hero's welcome and the Freedom of Norwich.

Sgt Harry Cator VC, MM, CdeG, was born on 24 January 1894. A modest man, he followed in his father's footsteps and worked on the railway at Drayton. Serving during the war with the 7th East Surreys, on 9 April 1917 he and his comrades went over the top near Arras, France. As the situation became desperate he advanced across No-Man's-Land picking up a Lewis gun and ammunition. He reached the enemy trench, knocked out its defences and held it, enabling the capture of 100 prisoners and five machine guns. For this courageous action he was awarded the Victoria Cross. Having been also decorated with the Military Medal and Croix de Guerre he was Norfolk's most decorated hero of the First World War.

47

Corporal Sidney James Day VC. Born in Norwich on 3 July 1891 he was educated at St Mark's School, Lakenham. He was awarded the VC for his gallant actions while serving with the 11th Battalion the Suffolk Regiment. On 26 August 1917 while his battalion was in Priel Wood, Malakoff Farm, east of Hargicourt, Day's section had cleared numerous enemy trenches. Upon his return a stick bomb fell into a nearby trench. Day seized it and hurled it back! After clearing this trench he remained at his post for 66 hours.

The tank leaving Norwich Market Place at the end of the city's Tank Week, 1–6 April 1918. The main purpose of Tank Week was to raise money for National War Bonds which were sold at £5 each in the 'Tank Bank' based in the Guildhall. Many stirring speeches were given from the tank – none more so than the musical performance crowned by Mlle Marcelle Moray, one of the last Belgian refugees to escape from Antwerp, who rendered an impassioned performance of *Brabanonne* with the *Marseillaise* as an encore. Tank Week raised £1,057,382 in Norwich alone.

A ghostly white shroud covers the Nurse Edith Cavell memorial shortly before it was unveiled by Queen Alexandra on 12 October 1918. The date was most poignant as it was three years to the day since she was executed by the Germans for 'conducting soldiers to the enemy'. Nurse Cavell is Norfolk's greatest heroine, and thousands crammed into Tombland to see her memorial unveiled. Annual services are still held by her grave at Life's Green, near the cathedral.

One almighty cheer goes up from the officers and men of the 51st and 52nd (Graduated) Battalion the Bedfordshire Regiment in Norwich Market Place. The time was the eleventh hour of the eleventh day of the eleventh month 1918. It was Armistice Day and the end of the First World War.

49

Officials and crew on one of the Anglo-Russian armoured cars beside the Guildhall on Norwich's Victory Loan Day, 8 July 1919. To the centre right of the picture in civilian clothes is Mr Peters from the National War Savings Association; to the right of him is Lt Moore who took charge of the cars in the absence of Commander Locker Lampson MP. Other speakers at the event included the Lord Mayor, the Rt Hon. G.H. Roberts MP and Lt-Commander Hilton-Young MP. This event saw Norwich raise £1,281,000 (£880,000 subscribed by the Norwich Fire & Life Offices) for the War Loan.

Hats returned after three cheers, the officers and men of the 2nd Battalion the Norfolk Regiment are officially welcomed home in Norwich Market Place, 11 April 1919. The 2nd Battalion had served with great distinction in the Middle East during the war, earning one of the most significant battle honours for the regiment at the Battle of Shaiba on 14 April 1915.

Between
the Wars

Norwich Peace Day celebrations, 19 July 1919. The Market Place is seen decked with the flags of all nations and squared by representatives of the fighting and civilian forces as Sir George Chamberlin delivers an address. In it he welcomed home our fighting forces, paid tribute to the war organisations and turned the thoughts of those assembled to those who did not return.

Although the country would never be quite the same again rural scenes began to be restored in the peace after the First World War. Here we see the Norwich Cattle Market in 1919. Behind the pens the backdrop is provided by Agricultural Hall Plain and Market Avenue. Some of the businesses seen along its length are the Plough and Jolly Farmers inns, Naggs and Greenacre's harness makers and Wicks sieve and screen makers.

The municipal buildings in Norwich Market Place, *c.* 1922. These buildings, at the turn of the century, were old public houses. From about 1910 the block was gradually purchased by Norwich City Council as committee rooms and administrative offices. Some of the old buildings were in a very poor state of repair – some rooms could not be used owing to unstable flooring, others had severe damp problems and it was, apparently, a constant battle to combat the rat infestation problems.

The employees of F.W. Harmer and Co. pile out from their factory (left) to completely block St Andrew's Street (a feat I would not wish to try today with modern traffic problems) to pose for the camera, *c.* 1922. They had worked hard throughout the war making uniforms for the fighting forces. In peacetime they returned to being family outfitters producing, among other items, 'Norvo' clothing for men, ladies' knitted outwear and 'Nunsuch' swimming suits. They were bombed out of their factory in 1942 and moved to a prefab factory in Heigham which served them until the Norwich branch of the company closed in the early 1990s.

Ready for the off! Members of the East Anglian Cycling Club and their 'starters' make ready for the first race of their club event at Norwich in the August Tuesday Sports of 1923.

Gentlemen's Walk, *c.* 1924. We see the jumble of market stalls on the right while in the foreground on the left is Howlett's musical instrument show rooms, Hope Brothers hosiers and outfitters, J. Lyons Refreshment Rooms with their affectionately remembered delicious cakes and 'nippies' (waitresses), H. Samuel the jewellers and finally Lloyds Bank.

Miss Ethel Mary Colman (1862–1948), Norwich's and indeed England's first Lady Lord Mayor who served her office in 1924. Ethel's constant companion, her sister Helen, acted as her Lady Mayoress. Descended from the great mustard-producing family, the sisters were a considerable influence on the city in the 1920s and '30s. They also restored and donated Stuart Hall and Suckling House to the city. Always shunning the attention their good works brought them and avoiding any ostentation it was said of them 'They had none of the fiercer characteristics of bluestockings . . . they were gentle but they did bear witness by the breadth of their own knowledge and interests to the depth of the Victorian culture in which they had been reared.'

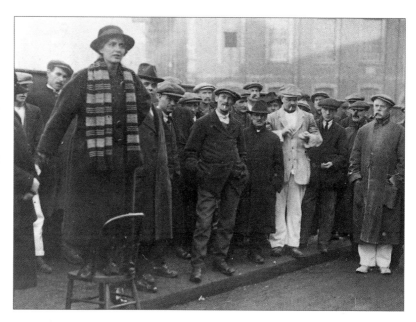

Miss Dorothy Jewson (1884–1964), prospective Labour MP for Norwich gives an address at J.J. Colman's Carrow Works 1923. It must have struck a chord as she was returned as MP the same year – the first woman in the city to attain the post. From 1925 to 1935 she represented the Eastern Division of the National Administrative Council of the Independent Labour Party and was a member of Norwich City Council from 1929 to 1936.

HRH Edward, Prince of Wales (later Edward VIII) opening Carrow Bridge on 27 June 1923. Norwich was without doubt one of the most proactive cities in tackling the unemployment problems of the 1920s and '30s and a number of public works were carried out across the city during that time. They were diverse schemes which ranged from laying out parks, building council housing estates (the first in England) and the redevelopment of the city centre. The Prince of Wales keenly supported this work and made no fewer than eleven visits to the city to open completed public works projects during the interwar years.

Two skilled craftsmen doing the hand-drawn work of inserting and finishing or 'making up' bristles into broom heads at Cook's Brush Works, Osborne Square on Timberhill in 1926.

The colonnade at Eaton Park under construction in 1924. Eaton, along with Wensum, Heigham, Woodrow Pilling, Hellesdon and Waterloo Parks were all laid down under the council employment schemes during the Depression. Opened by HRH Edward, Prince of Wales on 30 May 1928, Eaton Park was the largest of all the city parks created at this time. It covered 80 acres and had enough pitches, greens and courts to enable 600 people to be involved in organised games at any one time.

Eastern Evening News.

Registered for Transmission in the United Kingdom.

MONDAY, MAY 10th, 1926.

Price One Penny.

GENERAL NEWS.

SEVENTH DAY OF THE STRIKE.

MORE TRANSPORT IN LONDON.

There were improved train and bus services in practically all the districts of London this morning. The Executive of the Miners' Federation met early this morning. It is understood they considered the report of the conferences during the week end at Ostend of the Miners' International and the International Transport Workers' Federation, at which it is reported sympathetic strike action on the continent was rejected, and only a policy of an embargo on coal to England was decided upon.

Mr. Cook speaking in London last night declared they wanted a settlement and would make peace to-morrow if they could do it honourably. The terms were a living wage.

Mr. C.T.Cramp (N.U.R.) declared probably another of their big battalions would be thrown into the fighting line soon.

The Nonconformist Church in South Wales has passed a resolution urging the Government to reopen negotiations.

The Government declaration to all workers regarding their protection so far as Trade Union benefits are concerned which has been published in the "British Gazette" is to-day printed over the name of Stanley Baldwin. (See next column).

Young Middlesbrough hooligans destroyed scores of plate glass windows on Saturday. So menacing became the mob that the police charged with drawn batons dispersing the crowd.

The tramway strike in Bath is collapsing. 130 men reported for duty again this morning. This is practically half the total staff and services commenced on all 'ines at 10 o'clock. All the men are signing on as non-unionists.

Twenty-two persons were arrested as the result of week-end disturbances in Hull.

At High Mass in Westminster Cathedral yesterday Cardinal Bourne said that it was necessary Catholics should have before their minds the moral principles which were involved, namely:—(1) There was no moral justification for a general strike of this character. It was a direct challenge to lawfully constituted authority and inflicted injury on millions. It was therefore a sin against God who was the source of the authority. (2) All were bound to assist the Government, which in its own appointed sphere represented the authority of God himself. (3) It was the duty of all to pray for a lasting peace.

Two well known Labour leaders of Chopwell, County Durham, were arrested under the Emergency Act yesterday afternoon at Winlaton Mill. They were Mr. Will Lawther and Mr. Harry Bolton. Later they were charged at Felling Police Station and remanded, bail being refused.

FLIGHT OVER NORTH POLE.

A New York message says Lieut. Byrd, the American airman, yesterday flew over the North Pole and returned safely to Spitzbergen at 4.20 p.m., after a flight lasting 15½ hours.

LOCAL NEWS.

VOLUNTEERS AT NORWICH.

Mr. Herbert P. Gowen, Chairman of the Norwich Volunteer Services Committee states that there has been a very steady flow of volunteers each day, and Norwich compares in this direction favourably with all the big centres. The only trouble has been that there have been more applicants than work could be found for at the moment. Mr. Gowen, however, emphasised the fact that it was necessary that every person should enrol, so that they might be called upon as opportunity served.

A great need was special constables, and the Committee strongly appealed to eligible men to enrol as such at the Agricultural Hall.

Mr. Gowen in his capacity as Chairman of the Volunteer Services Committee caused the following circular to be affixed to tram standards in Norwich on Sunday morning:— "To all workers in all trades. Additional guarantees (official) Every man who does his duty by the Country and remains at work or returns to work during the present crisis will be protected by the State from loss of Trade Union benefits, superannuation allowances or pensions. His Majesty's Government will take whatever steps are necessary in Parliament or otherwise for this purpose.—STANLEY BALDWIN."

The Deputy Mayor informed us this morning that arrangements of the haulage committee were proceeding satisfactorily and, as far as the requirements of transport in the eastern area were concerned, haulage was being provided and co-ordinated for the service all essential commodities.

Several thousand Norwich citizens were present last evening at a united intercession service in St. Andrew's Hall. Canon Meyrick presided and was supported by the Lord Mayor, the Dean, Canon Aitkin, the Revs. Norman Hyde, C. T. Rae, J. J. Brooker, and other clergy and Nonconformist ministers.

Addressed by Mr. W. R. Smith and Mr. Mardy Jones, M.P. for Pontypridd, a demonstration attended by 10,000 or 12,000 trade unionists and others, was held at the Nest yesterday. The speakers strongly denied that the general strike is an attack on the authority of Parliament and the Constitution. Mr. Jones declared the breaking off of negotiations in consequence of what had happened at the "Daily Mail" office was a startling instance of Government stupidity. If negotiations had not been broken off then, the chances were that the general strike would never have taken place.

Girls and women who are unemployed or working short time, are invited to Samson and Hercules House, Norwich, free of charge and irrespective of membership of the Club, from 11 a.m. to 9.30 p.m. Canteen, recreation, etc.

A Special Cattle Train of 24 full trucks left Norwich Thorpe for London at 7.30 a.m. this morning.

Thirty boats delivered nearly 10 tons of fish to-day at Lowestoft. Prices fair, but fluctuated, mackerel 36/- per 100, herring £5 to £7 per cran.

Football:—Norfolk Charity Cup Final—Lynn 5, Yarmouth 1. Suffolk Charity Cup Final—Kirkley 4, Ipswich Works 1.

The cover of the *Eastern Evening News* from the seventh day of the General Strike, Monday 10 May 1926. With just about every business on 'walk-out' there was no daily paper published in the city on the 5th. After that papers appeared as an A1 sheet folded in half and printed on two sides. Even after the strike was officially declared 'off' on 12 May it was not until 15 May that the *Eastern Daily Press* reappeared in printed form as a newspaper.

The crowd strains at the ropes and necks are craned to observe the Norfolk & Norwich Aero Club plane enter Norwich Market Place, *c.* 1927. The club was founded in 1927. Its first solo flight from Mousehold Airfield was on 10 June that year and the pilot was Mr W. Moore of Great Yarmouth. The first air mail letter delivered to Norwich, addressed to Mr C.F Soloman, St John's House, Ber Street, followed three years later on 15 May 1931.

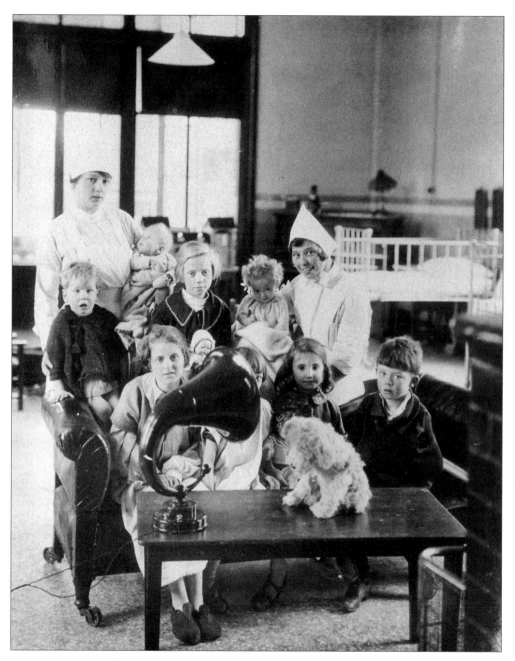

His master's voice? Children and their nurses listen to the radio at the Jenny Lind Hospital for Children, 1927. Approximately 1,500 children (boys up to ten and girls up to twelve years of age) were admitted and around 3,000 out-patients were treated annually in the 1920s and '30s. The cost of maintaining the hospital in those days was £8,000 per annum.

HRH Princess Mary opens the outpatients block at the Jenny Lind Children's Hospital, 29 June 1929. This event not only heralded the new but the closure of the original hospital buildings on Pottergate Street as all the hospital's business was now conducted at the Eaton site. The opening was not the only official engagement for Princess Mary as she went on to inspect the Norfolk County Rally of the British Red Cross Society at Crown Point.

Headmaster John William Howes and the boys of the Norman Endowed School, Cowgate, *c.* 1930. The school was probably unique in its foundation as it was begun by Alderman Norman in 1723 as a school for the sons related to himself or his first wife. The building seen here is the later schoolhouse which replaced the former one in 1839. The school was still endowed with about £1,000 a year and provided education for 85 scholars of the founder's kin. It closed in the early 1930s and the Mile Cross School was renamed the Norman School in his honour in January 1935.

The route is lined mostly by women and children and a sombre air descends on the city as it marks Armistice Day, c. 1930. They are waiting to see husbands, fathers, uncles and brothers march past on their way to lay wreaths and remember those who died in 'the War to end all Wars' at the ceremony held in front of the war memorial when it was at the end of the Guildhall.

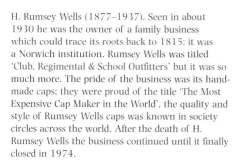

H. Rumsey Wells (1877–1937). Seen in about 1930 he was the owner of a family business which could trace its roots back to 1815: it was a Norwich institution. Rumsey Wells was titled 'Club, Regimental & School Outfitters' but it was so much more. The pride of the business was its hand-made caps; they were proud of the title 'The Most Expensive Cap Maker in the World', the quality and style of Rumsey Wells caps was known in society circles across the world. After the death of H. Rumsey Wells the business continued until it finally closed in 1974.

Marching out from their headquarters at the Lads' Club on King Street are the members of the 'Junior Police Force', *c.* 1930. The force was begun in about 1928 and was the brainchild of the Chief Constable, John Henry Dain, who also helped found the Lads' Club in Norwich. By the early '30s they were more popularly called 'carriage callers' because when they were on duty the most important task they performed was to whistle up carriages for guests after society events in the city.

'A very smart turnout all round' was the compliment paid to the members of the Norwich Lads' Club Division of the St John Ambulance Brigade by the Lord Mayor of Norwich after his inspection of the members in 1931. He was accompanied by their tireless leader, Superintendent Sidney Scott (far right) and Chief Constable John Henry Dain, just seen to Mr Scott's right.

Gymslips to the fore on the Norwich Girls' School Sports Day, held on the Newmarket Road ground, 1930. Sports days really were a feature of educational reforms in the years after the First World War. Events where both boys and girls of school age competed at separate games on the same field were still a rarity.

Trams on Orford Hill, c. 1931. By this time the death knell for the grand old tram system of Norwich was being sounded. Motor buses were beginning to run on the tram routes and a working agreement was announced between the United Bus Company and Eastern Motorways for bus services in East Anglia. In 1933 it emerged that Eastern Counties Omnibus Company had bought a controlling interest in the tramway company and they had begun the necessary legal procedures to bring about the abandonment of trams in Norwich.

The policeman, having sped to the scene (note he is still wearing his bicycle clips) surveys the damage at the steam lorry accident on Kett's Hill in October 1931. The lorry was one of the more familiar vehicles on the streets of the city as it was one of those owned by Edward J. Edwards, the well-known public works and sewerage contractors from Plumstead Road.

Having been declared unfit for Second Division matches the dear old 'Nest' ground of Norwich City Football Club was given up for the new ground at Carrow Road in 1934. One of the last matches, seen here in the thick of the action before a packed crowd, was one of the most unusual as it was played between speedway teams – on their bikes!

The Theatre Royal, 1934. Built as a concert hall by Thomas Ivory in 1758 it was later fully licensed as a theatre. In the early nineteenth century it was demolished and the new Theatre Royal was opened on 27 March 1826. In 1903 the theatre was sold to Messrs Bostock and Fitt and became the Hippodrome. Meanwhile the investment group led by Bostock and Fitt saw their long-term plan for a Grand Opera House on St Giles Street come to fruition. A few years later variety and music hall was all the vogue, the Grand Opera House became the Hippodrome and the Theatre Royal resumed its old name under its proprietor Mr Fred Morgan. The theatre buildings were destroyed by fire in 1934. It was reopened on 20 September 1935. Much of today's theatre is the result of its refurbishment and modernisation in 1971 and again in the early 1990s.

The Maddermarket Theatre, founded in 1921 by the great theatre man Nugent Monck. He raised £3,000 from supporters to buy the old chapel and baking powder factory as a home for his Norwich Players, turning the interior into a copy of an Elizabethan theatre for the performance of Shakespeare. The high quality of the performances, costumes and settings driven by Monck made the Norwich Players one of the most respected amateur groups in the country. Now providing a wide variety of theatrical performances and workshops the Maddermarket is still one of the most popular arts venues in the city.

Arthur 'Ginger' Sadd, 1914–22 (left) and one of his sparring partners at his Boxing Club for Lads, part of the Norwich Lads Club on King Street, *c.* 1935. Ginger's career as a professional boxer spanned 250 fights in nineteen years from 1932 to 1951. Renowned for his immaculate footwork and lightning fast left jab he was unbeaten in twenty fights up to 1938. He had won a number of bouts against top fighters like Freddy Mills, Pat Butler and Harry Mason. His greatest bout was, however, for the British Middleweight Championship which he lost on points against Jock McAvoy in May 1939.

Firemen inspect the burning embers in the shell of Hinde & Hardy's silk manufacturing factory on Botolph Street, Wednesday 24 October 1934. Within half an hour of the fire being discovered, at 2.00 a.m., the three-storey premises were reduced to a blazing shell. The city fire brigade attended but realised the factory, with all its flammable contents, could not be saved, so they concentrated on extinguishing the fire and limiting the damage to adjoining properties. The situation was brought under control after one-and-a-half hard fire-fighting hours.

Bunting and flags bedeck Rampant Horse Street, just one of the streets decorated for Jubilee Week which commenced on Jubilee Day, 6 May 1935. Other celebrations in the city included a grand street procession, the planting of a Davida tree at Earlham Park, band concerts in the public parks, a review of troops on the football field behind Britannia Barracks and a beacon built on St James's Hill by the Norwich Boy Scouts.

Girls from Avenue Road School, each with their partner ready to dance round the maypole, are part of the celebrations for King George V's Silver Jubilee, Monday 6 May 1935. Every child in city schools under the control of the Norwich Education Authority was presented with medallions and decorative souvenir boxes of chocolate toffees to celebrate the occasion.

The last tram to run along Earlham Road, 27 July 1937. This was also the last day for the Dereham Road route and was the beginning of the closure of the Norwich tramway system. The last ever tram ran on 10 December 1935 from Orford Place to the Silver Road tram sheds. As the packed tram departed it was cheered away and the crowd sang 'Auld Lang Syne'.

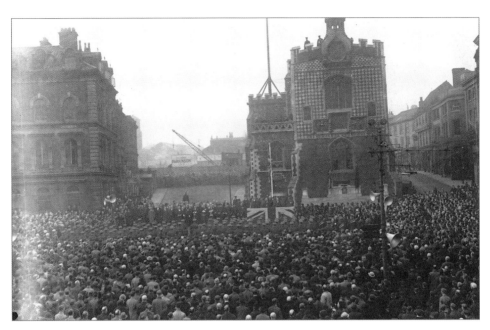

The King is dead, long live King Edward VIII is the proclamation read by Mr W.A. Riley, Lord Mayor of Norwich before a great crowd in front of the Guildhall on 22 January 1936. History was, however, not to see our new King crowned. In the background the crane and hoardings show that the demolition of St Peter's Road, part of the city centre redevelopment scheme, is in full swing.

A section of members from the City of Norwich Boys' Brigade march into Norwich Cathedral to pay their respects at the memorial service for George V, 28 January 1936. A great silence fell across the city, streets were deserted and shops closed as thousands crammed into the Market Place to listen to the funeral service in London over loudspeakers

Alfred Munnings (1878–1959) the region's most famous twentieth-century painter, renowned for his studies of country and equestrian sporting life, seen in 1935 on one of his many visits to Norwich. He came here at fourteen to train as a poster designer and studied each evening at the Norwich School of Art. The first of his 289 pictures which were to be exhibited by the Royal Academy was accepted in 1898. A spiritual kinsman of George Borrow he followed the gypsy life, and was known in his early life to sleep under their waggons in the pub yards of Norwich and its locality. In 1928 a retrospective exhibition of his work at Norwich Castle Museum attracted 86,000 visitors in six weeks. Elected president of the Royal Academy in 1944, he was knighted and given the Freedom of Norwich in 1947.

The Norwich Castle Time Ball photographed shortly before it was scrapped on 6 May 1938. First fired on 10 October 1900, it had outlived its purpose since the BBC time signals became so widely received via domestic radios. The Time Ball itself was electrically operated direct from Greenwich via the post office. The only human attention necessary was the daily insertion of the maroon a few minutes before the signal was due.

A close-up view of the Time Ball, shortly before it was dismantled in 1938.

What am I bid? The salvaged beams, slates and windows from St Peter's Road are auctioned off in front of the partially demolished municipal buildings on the Market Place. Part of the new city hall and city redevelopment scheme, houses had been purchased in this area since the late 1920s. When the buildings were being demolished a heaving brown mass emerged beneath the dust thrown up; as the mass dissipated it became apparent that it was swarms of rats, which took months to be properly eradicated from the area.

The statue of the Duke of Wellington, made by G.G. Adams and originally erected in Norwich Market Place in 1854, was moved as part of the city centre redevelopment scheme to Almary Green in the cathedral precincts in January 1937. Just before the 'Iron Duke' was fully restored to his plinth in the new location, we see the Lord Mayor of Norwich, Mr Herbert Frazer, placing a copper, tin-lined box containing the coins and documents found when the statue was moved, along with a copy of the *Eastern Daily Press* which charted the move, under the base on Wednesday 2 January 1937.

The Lord Mayor, Cllr W.A. Riley, wearing his chain and holding the trowel and Sir Ernest White (the councillor who deserves the credit for seeing the scheme through) with the gavel lay the inscribed foundation stone of Norwich City Hall on 24 September 1936.

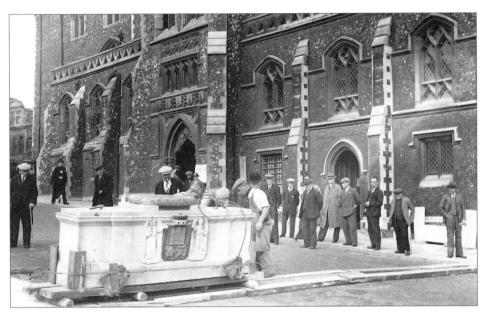

Moving the City of Norwich war memorial from its original position in front of the Guildhall, 1938. With Norwich's new City Hall nearing completion, efforts were concentrated on the redevelopment of the Market Place itself. The last of the old municipal buildings were demolished and a raised area between the City Hall and Market Place was created to become the city's War Memorial Gardens with the war memorial by Sir Edwin Lutyens RA as its centrepiece.

The finishing touches are applied by the Italian pavers to the new Market Place, declared at the time, 1938, to be '. . . one of the finest in all Europe'. The entire project of City Hall and Market Place redevelopment took three years and cost £222,000.

The opening night of the Odeon Cinema, Botolph Street, 7 February 1938. The Lord Mayor, Mr Charles Watling performed the official opening ceremony and the audience, which just about filled the 2,054 seats of the auditorium, settled down to watch *The Sky's the Limit*, a musical comedy, starring Jack Buchanan and Mara Loseff. The cinema lasted well into 1971 when it was demolished, and a new Odeon was built as part of the Anglia Square complex.

Saturday 29 October 1938: Bernard D. Storey, Town Clerk, leads the entourage of civic dignitaries and Royals from the Guildhall to the War Memorial Gardens where the memorial was re-dedicated in the presence of HM King George VI and Queen Elizabeth. The Royals then proceeded, in front of a crowd numbering many thousands, to open the new City Hall.

The
Second World War

Digging an air raid shelter on Chapel Field Gardens,
1938. With the winds of war blowing, the lessons of key
deployment of aircraft in the Spanish Civil War fuelled
peoples worst fears of complete destruction caused by air
raids. From late 1937 trenches and air raid shelters began
to spring up across the country.

Members of the City Works Engineers Department wearing their full anti-gas gear, *c.* 1939. Their job was to provide a fast response team to decontaminate areas where poison gas had been used. These were very real fears for the civilian population who had been issued gas masks from the late 1930s. Those who served in the First World War could speak of the horrific effects of poison gas in the trenches. Thank God it was not used on civilian targets in the Second World War.

Auxiliary firemen demonstrate how to tackle a fire with a bucket of water, stirrup pump and hose in front of the Agricultural Hall during Norwich's Civic Week, October 1938. What was due to be a week of civic festivities was overshadowed by Air Raid Precaution displays, march pasts and home defence services recruitment drives.

Children and parents can still raise a smile during an air raid drill where children file into the shelter at St Augustine's Council School in 1940. On the night of 27/28 April 1942 the school was destroyed by a 500kg bomb.

ARP Wardens of Group I, Division I, Post H, based at the children's home in Turners Road, Norwich, 1940. The wardens were volunteers, mostly from the St Benedicts/Dereham Road area. Trained since the late 1930s in all aspects of air-raid precautions, from stirrup pumps to gas masks, they will be best remembered for their stringent enforcement of the blackout with the call of 'Put that light out'.

The bus station viewed from Surrey Street and looking towards Queens Road after it was bombed in the third raid in the city, 30 July 1940. No alert had sounded at 6.00 a.m. as a Dornier 215 circled the city bombing from the River Wensum at Hellesdon, across Mile Cross Bridge and on to the bus station. One double decker bus was lifted off its front wheels and spun in ruins across the road while a second bus was totally wrecked. Luckily, this time, nobody was injured.

The NORWICH "SAFEGUARD"

An up-to-date War Time Handbook on matters and problems affecting the Emergency Life of the City and County

A.R.P. Instructions to the public.
Food Rationing.   First Aid Hints.
Black-out Tables for June and July.
War-Time Cookery Recipes, etc.
Allotment Holders' Page.
Words of advice from the A.R.P.
Controller for Norwich.

Published Bi-Monthly

By A. E. SOMAN & CO., LTD.
St. Andrews, Norwich

Wholesale Distributors: E. JOYCE & CO., LTD., St. Faith's Lane, Norwich

Norwich was quick off the mark to ensure its citizens were well informed about the facilities already in place with the war time handbook entitled *Safeguard*. Published as the war was coming dangerously close to home, this booklet included useful information on ARP services, rationing, war time cookery and first aid. There was also a pull out booklet listing the city's air raid shelters.

First Aid Party members at the Thorpe Depot, March 1941. Left to right: Miss Whyer, Ernie Fuller, 'Pop' Willsea, Ernie Mann, Bill Howsham and Harry Norton. Trained by pre-war serving members of the British Red Cross Society and St John Ambulance Brigade the job of FAPs was to work with the Civil Defence rescue teams to recover and give first aid to air raid casualties and, if necessary, transport them to hospital.

The members of the Steward & Patteson Auxiliary Fire Service, Patrol no. 21 in front of their shed at the Pockthorpe Brewery. Their vehicle is a converted truck which is loaded up with ladders, hose, rescue equipment and foam branch. The vehicle itself towed a Coventry Victor trailer pump.

Officers of the 4th Battalion the Royal Norfolk Regiment, *c.* 1940. Known as 'the Galloping Fourth' they were a territorial battalion with many of its officers, and the men they commanded, coming from Norwich. Their headquarters were the Drill Hall on Chapel Field. In 1941, after weathering one of the bitterest winters on record, on coastal defence duties, the 4th Battalion, along with the 5th and 6th, were sent to the opening war in the Far East. They went as part of the 18th (Eastern) Division. After distinguished fighting in the Straits of Johore they were forced back to Singapore Island. The allied forces were surrendered in February 1942 by General Percival and were then to endure the rest of the war in the living hell of forced labour, degradation and torture that was Japanese captivity.

Lt Patton RAMC places his stethoscope, cushioned by his handkerchief, against the side of the 1,000 lb bomb as it is carefully winched from its crater on Theatre Street, 24 September 1940. The bomb had been dropped in a raid a week earlier. It had been defused in hazardous conditions as it had struck a gas main when it buried itself in the road. This risky defusal and extraction was recognised by the presentation of a number of gallantry awards to the bomb disposal team.

City Engineers Department and utility emergency works squads get to work repairing and making safe the damaged houses and roadway on Caernarvon Road after the raid on the night of 30/31 March 1941. The bomb which landed here left a crater 10 feet across and damaged houses, water mains, gas mains and overhead telephone lines.

Members of the Norwich City Police Special Constabulary march past the Chief Constable and civic dignitaries on the steps of City Hall in April 1941. Note the steps and lamp posts are marked out with white edging or banding. This was done across Norwich to help those wending their way through the city in the blackout.

Motor Section of the 10th (City of Norwich) Battalion, Norfolk Home Guard. Photographed fully equipped in 1943 they were raised with the first units in May 1940 when they were known as the Local Defence Volunteers under Lt-Col B.F. Hornor DSO. The battalion had many achievements under its belt, among them the creation of a tank hunting platoon, Signal Company, a special unarmed combat squad. They even helped man the anti-aircraft defences of the city. At stand down in 1944 the unit strength was 113 officers and 2,495 other ranks.

Royal Observer Corps Norwich Centre no. 4 Crew, *c.* 1943. An often forgotten force of the Second World War, the Royal Observer Corps acted as the eyes of the RAF before radar. With various posts across the county they were able to plot the course of enemy raiders. Many of their number in Norwich came from the staff of the Norwich Union and many of the city centre shops that had vested interests in preserving their property. Many shops in the war years even had their own fire watchers armed with buckets, stirrup pumps and helmets. The work they did was, however, for the good of all and many lives were no doubt saved through the work of the ROC.

St Lawrence's Church silhouetted against the inferno of Norwich in flames during the night of 27/28 April 1942. This was to become known as the 'Baedeker Blitz' after the popular holiday guides that Hitler used to identify the significant historical sites across Great Britain as targets for his Luftwaffe in an attempt to break British morale.

The Wincarnis works and Odol factory, Westwick Street, on fire during the 'Baedeker Blitz' on Norwich on the night of 27 April 1942. When well-known Norwich photographer George Swain was taking this photograph the intensity of the flames scorched his camera.

Firemen still train their hoses on the burnt-out shops along Ber Street the morning after the raid of 27 June 1942. In the same area the well-known local drapery and houseware business of R.H. Bond & Sons Ltd was burnt out. Their premises incorporated the old Thatched Theatre which was also destroyed in this raid. Bond's were not to be beaten: they hired buses, parked them in the car park and used them as shops. Partly rebuilding their premises during the war, Bond's was eventually fully rebuilt, enlarged and is still known to shoppers in Norwich today.

The gardener's nightmare. An unexploded bomb in the garden of St Catherine's Plain on All Saints' Green, 3 November 1942.

Thousands crowd into Norwich city centre, bringing it to a halt, for the VE Day celebrations on 8 May 1945. However, VJ Day, signalling the end of hostilities in the jungles of the Far East and celebrated on 15 August 1945, was still two long months away, particularly for Japanese prisoners of war. For local service personnel it was to be another Christmas away from home before they actually returned to their beloved home county.

American Military Policemen or 'Snowdrops' form an honour guard on parade after the service in the cathedral to mark the end of the war, 1945. Joined on the parade by members of the military and home front forces they marched from Cathedral Close to City Hall where they passed the saluting dais draped with British and American flags.

Men representing all battalions of the Royal Norfolk Regiment on parade in front of City Hall when the regiment was granted the freedom of the city of Norwich, in recognition of the regiment's service over almost 250 years, particularly through two world wars, on 3 October 1945.

The
Postwar Years

Poor old Norwich, viewed from the castle mount, beaten and scarred by war. It would take a lot to rebuild it but the spirit and mettle which brought the Norwich people through the darkest days of the 'Baedeker Blitz' would see the city rise again.

The bottling stores, Morgan's Brewery, September 1948. One girl feeds the machine with empty bottles which are then washed and go to the girls in the foreground. The first girl is checking them to make sure they are clean and the next is making sure there are no breakages and stopping the machine if there are.

The bulging Christmas mail and parcel sacks arrive at the Norwich Royal Mail Sorting Depot. *c.* 1949. As ever additional staff were drafted in to deal with the extra workload. In the main they were young students on holiday or good old boys wanting a bit of extra money for the festive season.

One of the machine rooms of James Southall
& Co. Ltd, *c.* 1950. The business itself can trace
its origins back to the seventeenth century with
shops and factories in and around the Market
Place. In 1907 as the city grew Southalls
decided to move out to Crome Road. This
new factory was all on ground level covering
62,000 sq. feet. Today the business is simply
known as Start-Rite, after their most famous
product – the Start-Rite child's shoe.

Hindes' St Mary's Works Silk Mill, Oak Street,
c. 1950. The business was founded in 1810
by Ephraim Hinde. It was built up by his son
Francis and Francis's sons Frank and
C. Fountain who saw the purchase of Mills
at Mile Cross in 1927 and Oulton Broad and
1935. During the blitz of 1942 St Mary's
Works was so badly damaged it was out of
action for a number of months but working
double shifts at Mile Cross all war contracts
were still met. After the war they continued to
export all over the world. Sadly they closed in
1965 and as the last silk mill left in the city
they brought over 600 years of silk production
to an end in Norwich.

Sir Edmund Bacon, HM Lord Lieutenant for Norfolk, unveils the war memorial and opens the Royal Norfolk Regiment cottages on Mousehold Lane in 1951. The cottages were built as a memorial to the 2,025 officers and men of the Royal Norfolk Regiment who fell during the Second World War, and provided homes for deserving veterans.

'The Norfolkman' train, Thorpe station, *c.* 1950. Along with its 'brothers and sisters' with names like 'The Fenman', 'The Eastern Belle' and 'The East Anglian', these were the great trains which brought holidaymakers by the thousand from the north and London to the county. As demand on the old guesthouses grew during this period the coastline of Norfolk saw the vast expansion of holiday camps to accommodate our many visitors.

One of the Royal Artillery Searchlight crews which made the impressive displays at Norwich's Festival of Britain celebrations in June 1951 possible. As an encore for each day's festivities, concerts and displays, the spotlights were crossed over the spire of Norwich Cathedral thus dramatically illuminating it to become a great beacon, visible for miles around.

State trumpeters followed by members of the Household Cavalry trot into the grand ring at the Royal Norfolk Show, part of the celebrations for the Festival of Britain, 1951.

Here are some unusual visitors for the children at the Jenny Lind Hospital, *c.* 1951. These baby elephants were part of a travelling circus which was appearing at the Hippodrome and they called in at the hospital during their morning exercise.

Boys from the Cadet Norfolk Artillery demonstrate the no. 4 Lee-Enfield rifle on its sighting stand for Leonard Howes, Sheriff of Norwich, 1952. The CNA was formed in 1911 under the energetic leadership of Colonel R.C.O. Crosskill. During the Second World War membership was at its highest with 21 officers and 900 cadets. With the management of CNA cadets across Norfolk proving a problem it was at this time (1942) that membership of CNA was limited to the city of Norwich. The Cadet Norfolk Artillery still exists today as part of Norfolk Army Cadet Force.

Some of the 450 officers and men of the 1st Battalion the Royal Norfolk Regiment march past City Hall in sixes as Lt-Col Sir Edmund Bacon Bt, Her Majesty's Lord Lieutenant of Norfolk takes the salute on the occasion of the Battalion's 'Welcome Home from Korea' parade, 15 December 1954. This was probably the last occasion the Royal Norfolk Regiment marched, as their freedom right grants them, with 'bayonets fixed and bands playing' through the city of Norwich. The Royal Norfolk Regiment was amalgamated with the Suffolk Regiment as part of army reorganisation.

A scene from the Norfolk & Norwich Amateur Operatic Society's production of *Iolanthe*, performed at the Theatre Royal, March 1955.

What a display! Red Poll cattle fill the grand ring at the Royal Norfolk Show 1957. Truly part of Norfolk life in every way since it began in 1847, The Royal Norfolk Agricultural Association Show was itinerant for many years and was held at locations across the county including East Dereham. King's Lynn, Great Yarmouth and Diss. In 1953 it was held for the first time on land acquired specifically to house the great event at Costessey. All subsequent shows and numerous local events have been held on the site.

A policeman marshals shoppers across the zebra crossing during the Christmas rush on Gentleman's Walk in December 1957.

The Norwich Stars Speedway team, c. 1955. I wonder how many you recognise? Among them are the popular riders of the day like Phil Clarke, Aub Lawson and Billy Bales, not to mention the legendary Ove Fundin. These were the glorious days of Norwich Speedway at the Firs, Hellesdon, enjoyed by regular crowds of avid fans. The axe suddenly and tragically fell on the track when it was sold to become a housing estate in 1964.

Parade of over 1,000 members of the Norfolk branch of the British Red Cross Society in the grounds of their headquarters at Carrow Abbey, 1951. They were inspected by the Princess Royal and their senior county officers who all expressed themselves well pleased with the parade and commented on what a great pleasure it was to see many of those members who had served in the Second World War and who had maintained their membership after the end of hostilities.

Members of the Royal Norfolk Veterans Association gather in their club room on Redwell Street shortly before its closure in 1958. One of the first veterans associations it was formally founded in 1898 by Captain A.M. Atthill. Its charter was 'to rescue from the workhouse or pauper's grave any old soldier, sailor or marine who through no fault of his own is reduced to destitution'. Their good work was recognised in 1902 when Edward VII conferred the title 'royal' on the association. The group still exists today and enjoyed a reception with HM Queen Elizabeth at Sandringham on their 100th anniversary in 1998.

Brickies from Messrs. J. Joungs, Notley & Sons, City Road, June 1959. After the war the city licked its wounds and gradually pulled itself into order although there were still large bomb sites well into the 1960s. The city plan of 1945 took twenty years; efforts were concentrated more on building homes for bombed-out families or replacing the prefabs in the suburbs.

The Swinging
'60s & '70s

In February 1959 the City Station of the Midland & Great Northern Railway, along with the rest of the M&GN network, officially closed to passengers. In October 1960 the Midland & Great Northern Joint Railway Society laid on one of the last tours of this and the Waveney Valley lines. The lines were used for a few years more for freight but the station site was totally demolished and cleared in 1971.

A sight, sadly, never to be seen again: a Steward & Patteson's dray in front of the Black Horse on St Giles Street, *c.* 1960. On the dray is the beehive advertising S&P Honeysuckle Ale, remembered as a favourite tipple for the ladies. By the early 1970s Steward & Patterson had been bought out while the Black Horse pub and the Hippodrome Theatre beside it were reduced to rubble to make way for a car park and modern shops.

Crates of Bullards beer ready for the off from their Anchor Quay Brewery, July 1960. Bullards had been brewers in Norwich since 1837, most of that time on this same site, and up to the 1960s was still in Bullard family hands. They employed about 250 staff at the time, their proud boast being that at Christmas time over one million bottles of beer left this brewery. Despite a gallant attempt to survive by joining forces with other local breweries they could not compete against the nationals and were bought out by Watneys. In 1966 the Anchor Brewery closed. Today it is a trendy complex of apartments and houses.

Police dog handler PC Donald Johnson with Karl, Norfolk's new police dog, December 1960. The dog, a sable alsation, had come straight from the Metropolitan Police Dog Training School. Although Karl was just one year old he got to grips with police work after a week settling down at PC Johnson's home in Old Catton.

The final touches are added to the exterior of the refurbished Norwood Rooms on Aylsham Road, September 1960. The official public opening evening was Saturday 8 October – 'a first partner and parties only dance' with double tickets at 12s. Part of the Mecca organisation, entertainment was provided on the first night by Cyril Glover and His Orchestra although the Chick Aplin Orchestra are probably best remembered for their performances there over the ensuing years. Still in the hands of Mecca, the whole club is now a bingo hall.

Mr Jack Kiddell, who drove Frank Price's first motor vehicle in 1914 and was still driving for the firm when it closed down in September 1963.

The new high-speed automatic letter-sorting machine which was installed at the Norwich Post Sorting Office, January 1966.

Band Sergeant Baker puts some of the brass players from the 4th Battalion, the Royal Norfolk Regiment (TA) Band, through their paces, March 1964. Although the Royal Norfolk Regiment was amalgamated with the Suffolk Regiment to create the East Anglian Regiment in 1959, the Territorial battalions retained the title and badges of the old regiments. This was gradually phased out and in 1970 the Britannia cap badge was replaced by the star and castle of the Royal Anglian Regiment for all battalions.

Throughout the 1950s and '60s there was one venue synonymous with traditional live jazz performance – the Jolly Butchers on Ber Street. The atmosphere inside was legendary and was only possible in the years before stringent fire regulations. Take a floor area about 15 feet square, squeeze a band in and then pack the pub to the gills with standing room only. The experience was crowned by the landlady, the unforgettable Antoinette Hannent (1905–76). Known to all as 'Black Anna', she is seen here in about 1965, giving her all to a song in her inimitable way.

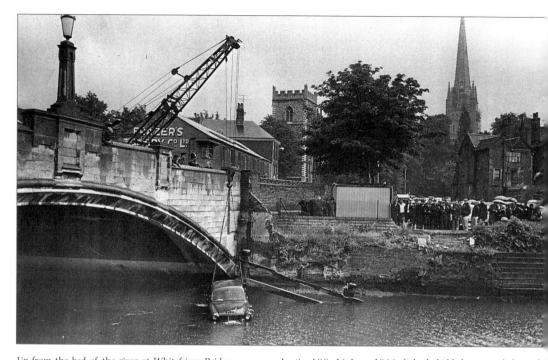

Up from the bed of the river at Whitefriars Bridge comes an Austin A90, 16 June 1966. It had skidded, careered through a wall and a fence (where the crowd is standing) and plunged into the water. The driver, twenty-eight-year-old Patrick McCarthy of 21 Yarmouth Road, was lucky to escape from the immersed car – he claimed he had no idea how he got out and confessed that he could not swim!

Colonel Sir Eric St Johnston, HM Inspector of Constabulary, inspects one of the last parades of the Norwich City Police Force, August 1967. Until 1948 Norwich, Great Yarmouth Borough and King's Lynn had their own police forces while county areas were covered by Norfolk County Constabulary. In 1948 King's Lynn was absorbed into the county and in 1966 it was announced the remaining three would amalgamate. Among a great deal of sadness, on 1 January 1968 the city and borough forces were no more.

Under the expert eyes of senior brewery workers the last ever brew is prepared at Steward & Patterson's Pockthorpe Brewery, January 1970. S&P had bought up a number of breweries in the city over the years and were the last of the 'classic' old-established Norwich breweries to close after they were bought out by Watney's in the late 1960s. The Pockthorpe Brewery was completely demolished by 1974 and now has houses and flats built on its site.

Hose reels sprawled across London Street give some idea of the fight to control the fire at Garlands Department Store, 1 August 1970. Garlands, which could trace its history in Norwich back to 1862, was closed for three years for reconstruction and refurbishment. It rose from the embers but never really recovered its business and closed for the last time in 1984.

103

Magdalen Street and Stump Cross, *c.* 1970. After the Second World War Magdalen Street enjoyed something of a revival as some of the shops whose frontages had begun to look tired were restored to their former glory and were occupied with a rich variety of businesses selling traditional and new products. The fortunes of the area, once so popular for shopping, appeared to be on the mend. Then some bright spark at an official level decided to put a flyover carrying the inner link road straight through the middle.

The sign says it all: the swathe has been cut through Magdalen Street with the flyover we see here under construction in 1971. In the same act just about all the shops and houses of Botolph Street, Calvert Street, Pitt Street and St George's Street were demolished to make way for a concrete shopping precinct, office blocks, car parks, cinema and more inner link road.

Eighteen-year-old Sally Phizackerley who had just finished her A levels is seen carefully clearing the soil from a skeleton found on the dig site behind St Andrew's Hall, 18 September 1974. With all the changes over the years Norwich has been blessed with a resident Archaeological Unit who have investigated, recorded and interpreted many sites of historical importance uncovered by demolition and change.

Brothers Ian and Stephen Greenfield enjoy a corner of the paradise for train and railway enthusiasts at the Norwich and District Model Engineers exhibition at Wensum Lodge, April 1975.

The Market Place is filled with flags and smiles as the crowd eagerly awaits the arrival of Queen Elizabeth II at City Hall while on her visit to the city, 11 April 1975.

The winner and runners up of the Miss Norwich competition held at the Earlham Park Mammoth Fete, August 1975. They are, left to right: Janet Usher from Wisbech (3rd), Miss Norwich 1975 Jackie Simmonds from West Wickham, Kent and Carolyn Grey from Norwich (2nd).

Pamela Boaden, Miss Snap 1976, releases the first balloon of the festival's great balloon race from its start on the Haymarket, 28 May 1976. The lucky finder of the balloon which had travelled the greatest distance won the first prize of £20 and two complimentary tickets to the Theatre Royal.

And they're off! The No. 1 entry in the Norwich raft race leaves Bishop's Bridge on 6 June 1977. This was just one of the events, entertainments and occasions hosted in the city to celebrate the Queen's Silver Jubilee.

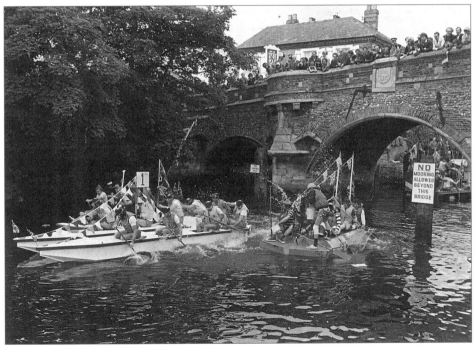

Whether you are an ardent churchgoer or not, your local clergy may well be known to you, not just because they hold religious office but because they are such great characters. This photograph includes some of the best remembered Norfolk clergy of the late twentieth century. Pictured shortly after their installation at Norwich Cathedral on 15 July 1977 are four new Canons and the officiating ministers. Left to right: the Bishop of Lynn Rt Rev. Aubrey Aitkin; Canon Derek Osbourne; Canon Maurice Burrell; Bishop of Norwich, the Rt Rev. Maurice Wood; Dean of Norwich, the Very Rev. Alan Webster; Canon Alan Glendenning and Canon David Maurice.

The newly opened Sainsbury Centre with its architect Mr (now Sir) Norman Foster, April 1978. The structure is over 400 feet long, 34 feet high and 115 feet wide with a gleaming outer skin. It stands at the westernmost point of the University of East Anglia campus at Earlham. The centre houses the modern, primitive and tribal art collection of Sir Robert and Lady Sainsbury which they presented to the university in 1973. Their son David gave a £3 million endowment at the same time to build the centre and add to the collection. The Sainsbury's donation has been compared with those of Ashmole to Oxford and Fitzwilliam to Cambridge. The centre itself has been compared to an aircraft hangar.

In a scene from the Norwich Passion Play, Jesus is comforted as he carries his cross. Opening on Friday 3 February 1978, the play was revived to mark the centenary of the birth of the theatre's founder, Nugent Monck, who devised the play in 1939.

No wonder they were smiling: this is the Angel Road team who became the first ever school to win all three major trophies in the Norwich Middle School Sports meeting at Lakenham in July 1977. Holding the shields are team captains Lorraine Reeve (left) and Andrew Quantrell.

The brick and tile St Ethelberts, known as 'Boswell's Restaurant', photographed after being engulfed with flames on 11 June 1978. It took over three hours to bring it under control and sixty firemen fought the blaze wearing breathing apparatus, to enable them to gain access through the blankets of smoke in the three storeys of the burning building. With buildings either side, there was no way to quell the flames other than by cutting a hole through the tiled roof. The owner, former American war correspondent Hy Kurzner sat on a Tombland bench observing the devastation. Asked if he would rebuilt it he replied '. . . Damn right I will' – and he did.

Three of the forty firemen who fought the 'tinder-box' fire at Hovells on Bridewell Alley, 8 November 1978. The first firemen on the scene were from Sprowston fire station on Chartwell Road who arrived eight minutes after the call was received. The fire took two hours to be brought under control; the pall of smoke from the blaze at its height could be seen a couple of miles away. Although reduced to a shell, Hovells Basket Shop was restored and is still trading today.

Modern Times

The Anti-nuclear protest which marched from City Hall to Bawburgh underground government shelter, 13 December 1980. This was just one of many such demonstrations throughout Britain to mark the anniversary of the decision to site Cruise and Pershing II missiles in Europe.

Members of the original BBC Radio Norfolk team gather for the camera on top of Norfolk Tower shortly before the launch of the station in September 1980. This was just one of the stations which spearheaded the BBC initiative to provide local radio stations to serve whole counties rather than just city centres. In the early years they only broadcast for a few hours each day, providing a breakfast show and news bulletins, with Radio 2 as a sustaining service. As Radio Norfolk developed, the station has always striven to involve local people and to provide programmes with a county-wide appeal. Because of this innovation and commitment it has been taken to the hearts of Norfolk people, and remains one of the most popular stations of its kind in the country.

The opening of Bewlay's tobacconist shop on Gentleman's Walk, January 1981. The shop was launched by a retinue of characters in mock-eighteenth-century costume led by Mr Ted Wilson, from Great Dunmow, Essex, four times national champion town crier, who opened proceedings in his own unmistakable manner.

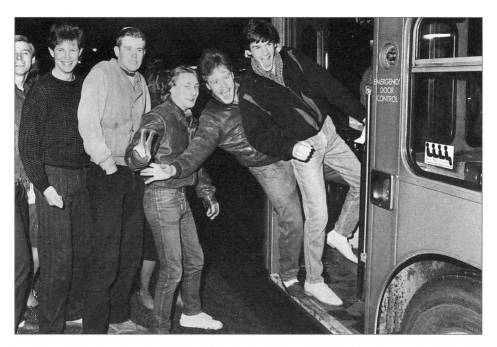

The 'Boozer Cruiser' service set up in Norwich during the festive period, 1984. The idea was that late night buses could pick up and later return revellers to help avoid drinking and driving as well as bad behaviour on the streets after hours.

Firemen hose down the smouldering remains of the boardroom of Norwich City Football Club, 25 October 1984. The fire, discovered shortly after 3 a.m., engulfed the whole of the main stand. Over 30 firemen with their tenders from Norwich, Hethersett, Sprowston and Wymondham fought for several hours to bring it under control. Although the stand was soon rebuilt the historical silver cups and pennants from the boardroom were twisted or lost altogether in the fire.

Robotronix, 1988. This distinctive pair entertain passers-by in the street by moving and performing simple tasks to music in the character of life-size robots. I remember them well; they were fascinating to watch. Norwich has a wonderful diversity of street entertainers such as Joe Dade the underpass accordionist, guitarists, skiffle bands and even the occasional string quartet.

Any of us who remember Norwich in the 1980s must recall this image. The no. 26 bus to Hellesdon was travelling along Earlham Road when the ground literally opened up beneath it as an old chalk working gave way on 3 March 1988. Tributes were paid to the driver Jimmy Pightling who remained calm and assisted passengers off as the bus sank into the 30 foot deep cavern.

The new Anglia News team of Fenella Hadingham, John Bacon, Helen McDermott and John Francis, 6 July 1990. This heralded the last *About Anglia* which was first presented by Dick Joice in May 1960. The 30-year-old programme gave way to *Anglia News*, a £2 million dual news service supplying viewers in the east and west of the region with separate bulletins.

Overtime Easter egg line at Nestlé in January 1990, eighteen months after the Rowntree Mackintosh factory had been taken over by the giant Swiss firm. At the time the plant was working day and night until February, when in this one season they would have made 35 million chocolate eggs. Nobody could have imagined the factory would be closed by Nestlé as part of a cost-cutting exercise in December 1994, with the loss of 900 jobs.

Charles Roberts and Theatre Royal Chaplain, David Sharp, raise a glass as a familiar face returns to the Theatre Royal, 5 November 1992. The face unveiled at a simple ceremony was that of 'Mr Theatre Royal' Dick Condon, the general manager. His portrait returned in the form of a painting by local artist Gareth Hawker and was hung in the theatre's Long Gallery.

Interior view of the Castle Mall Shopping Centre which was completed in September 1993. The mall development occupies nearly 7 acres in the centre of Norwich. The complete scheme took almost ten years to develop and build. Construction cost £75 million with a total development cost of £145 million. With over 380,000 sq. feet of retail space and now even a multiplex cinema it provides a fine additional trade centre for the city.

Children attempt to hoop the bottles at the twelfth annual Mile Cross Festival, 2 July 1994. Hosted in and around the Norman Centre there were displays from the Norwich Fire Cadets, country dancing by Norman First School and the Phoenix Carnival Club. This is a real Mile Cross event with most of the entertainment provided by local residents.

Fire crackers bang and crackle and cymbals crash as the dragon performs outside City Hall, and the onlookers share in the spectacle of celebrating the Chinese New Year, 31 January 1995. The display was mounted as part of the Norwich 800 Celebrations (May 1994–May 1995) which marked the city's charter for self-government signed by Richard 1 in 1194.

Jugglers gather in front of City Hall, 22 April 1995. Jugglers had come from all over Britain for the Eighth National Juggling Convention, hosted this year in Norwich. They provided a street parade through the city and gave demonstrations on Chapel Field Gardens, culminating in a variety show at the Lads' Club on King Street.

The streets of Norwich have seen some unusual sights in their time. Norfolk has a great history of religious nonconformity but I bet the county has still not seen too many Tibetan monks, seen here on their visit to the city, 19 May 1995.

Smiles all round from the 35th Norwich Sea Scouts, Cubs and Beavers with their new tent, 18 June 1997. As time goes on membership of many youth groups has sadly fallen while the cost of running such groups. It is very refreshing to see that when these youngsters wanted a 10-berth tent for their expeditions they used their initiative and approached a building society for help. They paid for it and Tina Cohen, manageress of the N&P Castle Mall branch, is seen to the left after presentation of the tent.

Fire crews attempt to quell the blaze at the Norwich Central Library, 1 August 1994. Not only was the lending library destroyed but so was the American Memorial Library and a large proportion of the Local Studies Library. The burnt-out shell and images of the charred and water-damaged volumes of Norfolk's history will haunt anyone who saw it.

In the year 2000, out of the charred remnants of the old library and Bethel Street car park comes the phoenix of the new libraries and information centre which has been adopted as the Norfolk & Norwich Millennium Project. Local citizens and local historians have worked hard to reconstitute what was lost in the Local Studies Library; their collection is also growing anew. We all look forward to seeing the new facility open in 2001.

Norwich City Hall, 2000. Still the lofty marble-lined hall that is the administrative centre of the city; on a still night the chimes of its clock may be heard right across the city. Royal visitors including George VI, Queen Elizabeth the Queen Mother and Queen Elizabeth II have all visited. Many civic occasions have been centred here from annual march-pasts to events such as 'Salute the Soldier' and 'Norwich 800'. It was also here that the city's millennium night celebrations were hosted. The revellers watched the countdown to the new millennium projected on to Norwich Castle from here. I wonder what it will see in the next 100 years?

Norwich City viewed from Mousehold, 2000.

Acknowledgements

I would like to extend my personal thanks to the following who have so generously contributed images, information and memories to make this book possible: Basil Gowen, Philip Standley, George Plunkett, the staff and library of the *Eastern Daily Press*, Captain Philip Watson of the 9th/12th Royal Lancers (Prince of Wales's), Andy Archer, Maggie Secker and all contributing listeners of BBC Radio Norfolk, Geoffrey Kelly for his detailed information on 'Black Anna' and Terry Burchell for the usual photographic wonders.

A very special thanks must be given to my friends at the Norfolk Local Studies Library for their patience, fortitude and diligence in helping me with even the most obscure of enquiries. This standard of service is not unique to me; I am convinced they freely share this remarkable co-operation with any who call upon their assistance. They are all a credit to their profession.

Whenever I begin to think the unusual photographs are drying up, or as I begin to research another historical topic, I never cease to be surprised and delighted by what is 'out there' tucked away in the albums and cupboards of Norfolk households. Without the ongoing contribution of the people of Norfolk my books would not exist. I have never been let down in my quest for 'just one more photograph' so I send a very genuine and heartfelt thanks to those people, too numerous to mention, who have been so very kind to me over the years.

Finally, but by no means least, I wish to thank my family, old and new, especially my darling wife Sarah for her additional research work and love for this temperamental author.

Every attempt has been made to obtain permission to reproduce the images herein. If there are any omissions in my acknowledgements please forgive me as no breach of those rights was intended.